THE RESILIENCE FACTOR

TRANSFORMING SETBACKS INTO STEPPING STONES

DR. MINAKSHI BANSAL

Copyright © Dr. Minakshi Bansal
All Rights Reserved.

This book has been self-published with all reasonable efforts taken to make the material error-free by the author. No part of this book shall be used, reproduced in any manner whatsoever without written permission from the author, except in the case of brief quotations embodied in critical articles and reviews.

The Author of this book is solely responsible and liable for its content including but not limited to the views, representations, descriptions, statements, information, opinions and references ["Content"]. The Content of this book shall not constitute or be construed or deemed to reflect the opinion or expression of the Publisher or Editor. Neither the Publisher nor Editor endorse or approve the Content of this book or guarantee the reliability, accuracy or completeness of the Content published herein and do not make any representations or warranties of any kind, express or implied, including but not limited to the implied warranties of merchantability, fitness for a particular purpose. The Publisher and Editor shall not be liable whatsoever for any errors, omissions, whether such errors or omissions result from negligence, accident, or any other cause or claims for loss or damages of any kind, including without limitation, indirect or consequential loss or damage arising out of use, inability to use, or about the reliability, accuracy or sufficiency of the information contained in this book.

Made with ♥ on the Notion Press Platform
www.notionpress.com

DEDICATION

To my children, who inspire me every day to be the most resilient version of myself. May you always embrace life's challenges with courage, curiosity, and an unwavering spirit.

ᗷᗷᗷ

Contents

Contents

Contents

Prayer

"Om Bhadram Karnebhih Shrinuyama Devah

Bhadram Pashyemakshabhiryajatrah

Sthirairangais Tushtuvamsastanubhih

Vyashema Devahitam Yadayuh

Svasti Na Indro Vriddhashravah

Svasti Nah Pusha Vishwavedah

Svasti Nastarkshyo Arishtanemih

Svasti No Brihaspatir Dadhatu

Om Shantih Shantih Shantih"

This mantra is a prayer for universal well-being, invoking the blessings of various deities for protection, health, and happiness. It emphasizes the importance of experiencing the auspicious through all senses and living a life aligned with divine purpose. The repetition of "Shantih" at the end signifies a deep desire for peace in the individual, the environment, and the universe at large. This mantra is often recited as a prayer for peace, prosperity, and the physical and spiritual well-being of all beings.

ॐॐॐ

"

About The Author

This book represents the culmination of extensive research and meticulous analysis, incorporating a diverse range of sources, including numerous books, scholarly studies, and personal experiences. Additionally, I have scoured various websites to gather relevant information and data essential for the compilation of this work. I have taken every precaution to ensure the accuracy of the information presented and have diligently cited all sources to acknowledge their contributions.

From her earliest days, Minakshi was distinguished by an insatiable appetite for reading. Her literary universe was inhabited by characters and narratives that spanned ethical tales, motivational and inspirational stories, and the mythic parables imbued with life lessons. This voracious reading habit was not merely for personal edification but was driven by a desire to distill and disseminate the essence of these narratives to foster the development of students and peers alike. She was particularly captivated by the lives and teachings of historical figures and spiritual leaders such as Adi Shankaracharya, Swami Vivekananda, Dr. APJ Abdul Kalam, Mahamana Pandit Madan Mohan Malviya, Mahatma Gandhi, Sardar Vallabhai Patel, and Vinoba Bhave, among others. Their philosophies and life stories fueled her ambition to embody their ideals of resilience, selflessness, and relentless pursuit of knowledge.

Dr. Minakshi's academic and practical engagement with psychology has been equally noteworthy. As a research scholar, her focus has been on exploring the intricate tapestry of the human psyche, aiming to unlock the potential for psychological well-being and societal harmony. Her scholarly work is complemented by her active involvement in social work, where she employs her academic insights to make tangible differences in the lives of the underprivileged. Her endeavours in social work are characterized by an innovative approach that combines traditional wisdom with contemporary psychological practices to address the multifaceted challenges faced by these communities.

Her artistic talents, another facet of her diverse capabilities, are not merely a personal passion but also serve as a medium through which she communicates and connects with others. Her art, rich in symbolism and emotional depth, reflects her philosophical inquiries and social concerns, offering viewers a glimpse into the breadth of her intellect and the depth of her compassion.

In addition to her contributions to the arts and social sciences, Dr. Minakshi has embraced the healing arts of Pranic Healing, mastering the techniques developed by Master Choa Kok Sui. This practice, which focuses on the manipulation of Prana or life energy to heal the body and aura, has been both a personal journey of discovery and a means through which she extends her healing touch to others. Her proficiency in Pranic Healing is complemented by her advocacy and teaching of various forms of meditation aimed at rejuvenation, personal betterment, and the cultivation of harmony within individuals and communities alike.

Dr. Minakshi's life is a narrative of relentless pursuit, not just of personal achievement but of the upliftment and empowerment of society at large. Her diverse interests and talents—spanning the arts, literature, psychology, and the healing practices—converge on a singular path of service. She embodies the spirit of the luminaries who inspired her, channelling their legacy through her actions and teachings. Through her books, art, and social initiatives, she continues to inspire a new generation to embark on their own journeys of self-discovery, resilience, and altruism.

Her commitment to social betterment, particularly her focus on uplifting underprivileged children, reflects a deep understanding of the transformative potential of education and personal development. By integrating her knowledge of psychology, her artistic sensibilities, and her healing practices, Dr. Bansal has developed a holistic approach to social work that addresses both the immediate needs and the long-term well-being of the communities she serves.

As an author, Dr. Minakshi's writings offer a blend of inspirational insights, practical wisdom, and reflective contemplations drawn from her extensive reading and life experiences. Her books serve as a guide for those seeking to navigate the complexities of life with grace, resilience, and purpose. Through her narratives, she extends an invitation to her readers to explore the depths of their own potential and to contribute meaningfully to the collective well-being of society.

In Dr. Minakshi Bansal, we find a remarkable synthesis of the artist, the scholar, the healer, and the social activist. Her life's work stands as a beacon of hope and a source of inspiration for individuals seeking to make a difference in the world. Her story is a compelling reminder of the power of individual action, rooted in compassion and driven by a profound commitment to the betterment of humanity. Dr. Minakshi's legacy is not just in the tangible outcomes of her efforts but in the enduring spirit of inquiry, empathy, and service that she embodies.

ꕔꕔꕔ

Preface

In a world that constantly throws us curveballs, where life's unpredictable winds can knock us off our feet, resilience emerges as our anchor, our guiding light through the storms. This book is an invitation to embrace resilience, not as a distant ideal, but as a tangible, practical, and life-changing practice.

In the tapestry of my own life, I've encountered my fair share of challenges and setbacks. I've weathered storms of grief, navigated the choppy waters of career changes, and faced the inevitable bumps and bruises that come with raising a family. Through it all, resilience has been my unwavering companion, my compass guiding me through the darkest hours.

As a woman, I've often felt the pressure to be perfect, to juggle multiple roles with effortless grace, and to always put the needs of others before my own. But in my journey towards resilience, I've discovered the power of embracing imperfection, of recognizing that "good enough" is often better than perfect. I've learned that resilience is not about being superhuman; it's about being human. It's about acknowledging our vulnerabilities, embracing our emotions, seeking support, and learning from our experiences.

In this book, I share the lessons I've learned, the tools I've acquired, and the strategies I've developed to cultivate resilience in my own life. This is not a self-help book filled with empty platitudes or unrealistic expectations. It's a heartfelt invitation to embark on a journey of self-discovery, to explore the depths of your own resilience, and to unleash your inner strength.

In this book, we'll delve into the science of bouncing back, exploring how our brains and bodies are wired for resilience. We'll debunk common myths that hold us back and uncover the truth about what it really means to be resilient. We'll explore the power of mindset, the importance of self-compassion, and the art of emotional regulation.

We'll navigate the challenges of the modern workplace, building resilience in the face of demanding deadlines, difficult colleagues, and unexpected setbacks. We'll delve into the intricacies of relationships, learning how to navigate conflict, build stronger bonds, and foster a resilient connection with our loved ones. We'll even explore the unique challenges and rewards of parenting, discovering how to raise resilient children while staying sane ourselves.

This book is not just about surviving life's storms; it's about thriving in them. It's about creating a life that is not only successful but also meaningful, fulfilling, and resilient. It's about embracing challenges as opportunities for growth, setbacks as stepping stones, and adversity as a catalyst for transformation.

My hope is that this book will serve as a guide, a companion, and a source of inspiration on your journey towards resilience. May it empower you to embrace your imperfections, to celebrate your strengths, and to discover the boundless potential that lies within you. Remember, resilience is not a destination; it's a lifelong practice. Embrace the journey, and watch yourself blossom into the most resilient version of yourself.

Dr. Minakshi Bansal
Social Activist
Ahmedabad, Gujarat, Bharat

ᖋᖋᖋ

ONE

WHAT IS RESILIENCE, ANYWAY? DEMYSTIFYING THE CONCEPT AND WHY IT'S YOUR SECRET SUPERPOWER.

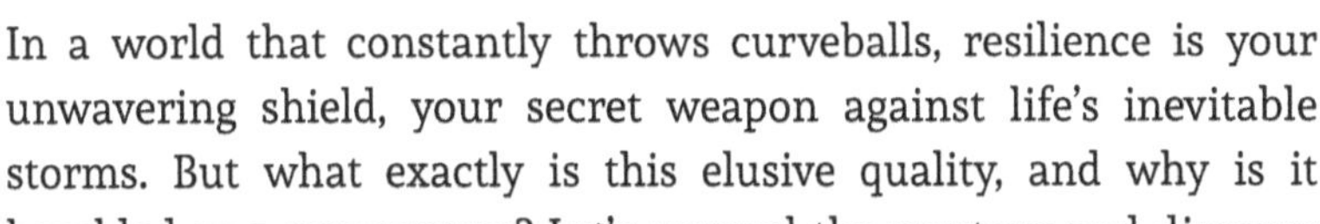

In a world that constantly throws curveballs, resilience is your unwavering shield, your secret weapon against life's inevitable storms. But what exactly is this elusive quality, and why is it heralded as a superpower? Let's unravel the mystery and discover how resilience can transform your life.

At its core, resilience isn't about avoiding difficulties or pretending they don't hurt. It's not about being unfeeling or stoic. Instead, resilience is the art of navigating life's challenges with grace, courage, and an unyielding spirit. It's about acknowledging the pain, the setbacks, and the disappointments, yet refusing to let them define you. Resilience is the ability to bend without breaking, to adapt, to learn, and to emerge from adversity even stronger than before.

Think of resilience as a muscle. Just as physical exercise strengthens your body, facing and overcoming challenges strengthens your resilience. It's not something you're born with or without; it's a skill you can cultivate, a mindset you can adopt, a habit you can develop. And the more you practice it, the stronger it becomes.

But why is resilience your secret superpower? Because it gives you the ability to thrive in the face of adversity. When life throws you a curveball, resilience allows you to catch it, analyze it, and use it to your advantage. It helps you find the silver lining in even the darkest clouds, the opportunity in every obstacle.

Resilience empowers you to take control of your life, to make choices that align with your values and goals, even when things get tough. It helps you stay focused, motivated, and determined, even when the going gets tough. With resilience, you become the captain of your own ship, navigating through stormy seas with confidence and composure.

Resilience isn't just about overcoming adversity; it's also about preventing it. By building your resilience, you become better equipped to handle stress, manage emotions, and maintain a positive outlook. This, in turn, protects you from the negative impacts of stress and adversity, reducing your risk of burnout, anxiety, and depression.

Resilience isn't just a personal asset; it's also a social one. When you're resilient, you become a beacon of hope for others, a source of inspiration and support. Your resilience can uplift those around you, encourage them to face their own challenges, and create a ripple effect of positive change.

The benefits of resilience are far-reaching. Studies have shown that resilient individuals tend to be happier, healthier, and more successful in various aspects of life. They have stronger relationships, greater job satisfaction, and a more positive outlook on life. Resilience is not just a survival skill; it's a thriving skill.

So, how can you cultivate resilience? Start by embracing a growth mindset, the belief that you can learn and grow from every experience, whether positive or negative. Challenge negative self-talk and replace it with positive affirmations. Focus on your strengths and accomplishments, and celebrate your small victories.

Practice self-care. Take care of your physical and mental health, prioritize sleep, exercise, and healthy eating. Find healthy ways to manage stress, such as meditation, yoga, or spending time in nature.

Build a strong support system. Surround yourself with positive, supportive people who believe in you and your ability to overcome challenges. Don't be afraid to ask for help when you need it. Remember, you don't have to go through life alone.

Finally, embrace challenges as opportunities for growth. Don't shy away from difficult situations; instead, see them as stepping stones on your path to success. With resilience, you can turn setbacks into comebacks, failures into lessons, and obstacles into opportunities.

Resilience is not an overnight transformation; it's a lifelong journey. It requires patience, perseverance, and a willingness to learn and grow. But the rewards are immeasurable. With resilience, you can not only survive life's storms, but you can also thrive in them. Remember, resilience is your secret superpower. Embrace it, cultivate it, and unleash your full potential.

❦❦❦

Resilience isn't about being immune to pain, but about finding the strength to dance with it. It's about embracing the full spectrum of human emotions and using them as fuel for growth and transformation.

TWO

THE RESILIENCE SPECTRUM: WHERE DO YOU FALL? DISCOVERING YOUR CURRENT RESILIENCE LEVEL.

The resilience spectrum isn't a rigid scale with a definitive start and end. Instead, it's a fluid, dynamic range of resilience levels that we fluctuate within throughout our lives. Picture it as a vibrant landscape, with rolling hills representing different challenges and valleys signifying moments of vulnerability. Where you stand on this spectrum isn't fixed; it's a reflection of your current state, influenced by various factors like your experiences, mindset, support system, and even your physical well-being.

Understanding where you fall on the resilience spectrum is an essential step in your journey toward greater resilience. It's like having a compass that guides you, revealing your strengths and areas for growth. So, how can you discover your current resilience level? Let's embark on a self-discovery expedition.

Reflecting on Past Experiences: Think back to a time when you faced a significant challenge or setback. How did you react? Did you feel overwhelmed and defeated, or did you find a way to cope and adapt? Did you seek support from others, or did you try to handle it all on your own? Your response to past challenges can provide valuable clues about your current resilience level.

Assessing Your Mindset: Your mindset plays a crucial role in your resilience. Do you tend to view challenges as threats or opportunities? Do you believe in your ability to overcome obstacles, or do you doubt yourself and your capabilities? A growth mindset, the belief that you can learn and grow from every experience, is a hallmark of high resilience.

Evaluating Your Support System: The people around you can significantly impact your resilience. Do you have a strong network of friends, family, or colleagues who you can rely on for support during tough times? Having a strong support system can bolster your resilience, providing you with a safe space to express your emotions, seek guidance, and receive encouragement.

Examining Your Emotional Regulation Skills: How well do you manage your emotions when faced with stress or adversity? Do you tend to react impulsively, or can you step back, assess the situation, and respond in a thoughtful and constructive manner? Emotional regulation is a key component of resilience, allowing you to stay calm and focused under pressure.

Considering Your Physical Well-being: Your physical health can also influence your resilience. Do you prioritize sleep, exercise, and healthy eating? When you're physically well, you're better equipped to handle stress and adversity. On the other hand, neglecting your physical health can deplete your energy and make it harder to bounce back from challenges.

As you reflect on these factors, you might notice patterns or tendencies. Perhaps you're naturally resilient in some areas but struggle in others. Maybe you've experienced significant growth in your resilience over time, or perhaps you feel like you've plateaued. Remember, there's no right or wrong place to be on the resilience spectrum. It's a personal journey, and everyone's path is unique.

Once you've identified your current resilience level, you can start setting goals for growth. Perhaps you want to improve your emotional regulation skills, strengthen your support system, or develop a more positive mindset. There are many resources available to help you build resilience, including books, workshops, therapy, and online courses.

Remember, building resilience is an ongoing process. It's not about achieving perfection, but rather about making progress. Celebrate your successes, learn from your setbacks, and be kind to yourself along the way. The journey toward greater resilience is a worthwhile one, leading you to a more fulfilling, empowered, and joyful life.

So, where do you fall on the resilience spectrum? Take the time to reflect, assess, and discover. Your resilience level isn't a static label; it's a dynamic reflection of your current state. By understanding where you stand, you can take intentional steps to cultivate greater resilience, transforming challenges into opportunities and setbacks into stepping stones. The journey toward resilience is a personal one, but it's a journey worth taking. Embrace it, and watch yourself blossom into a stronger, more resilient version of yourself.

❦❦❦

Your mindset is your most powerful asset. Embrace a growth mindset, where challenges become stepping stones and setbacks become opportunities to learn and evolve.

THREE

THE SCIENCE OF BOUNCING BACK: HOW YOUR BRAIN AND BODY ARE WIRED FOR RESILIENCE.

Resilience isn't just a mindset or a character trait; it's deeply rooted in the intricate workings of our brains and bodies. We are, in fact, biologically wired for resilience, equipped with an astonishing array of mechanisms that help us adapt, recover, and thrive in the face of adversity. Let's delve into the fascinating science behind bouncing back and discover how our own biology empowers us to overcome challenges.

At the heart of resilience lies neuroplasticity, the brain's remarkable ability to reorganize itself by forming new neural connections throughout life. When we encounter stress or adversity, our brains activate a cascade of responses, triggering the release of stress hormones like cortisol and adrenaline. These hormones prepare us for fight-or-flight, mobilizing energy and sharpening our focus. However, prolonged or excessive stress can have detrimental effects on our brains, impairing cognitive function and increasing our vulnerability to mental health issues.

Resilience, on the other hand, activates a different set of neural pathways. When we face challenges with a resilient mindset, our brains release neurochemicals like oxytocin and dopamine, which promote social bonding, reduce anxiety, and enhance our ability to learn and adapt. This neurochemical cocktail acts as a buffer against the negative effects of stress, protecting our brains and fostering resilience.

Neuroplasticity also allows us to reframe our experiences and find meaning in adversity. When we encounter setbacks, our brains can rewire themselves to focus on the positive aspects of the situation, identify potential opportunities for growth, and develop new coping strategies. This process of reframing and learning from experience is essential for building resilience.

The intricate dance between stress and resilience isn't confined to the brain; it extends to our entire body. When we experience stress, our bodies activate the sympathetic nervous system, triggering a host of physiological responses, such as increased heart rate, rapid breathing, and muscle tension. These responses prepare us for action, but if they persist for too long, they can take a toll on our health.

Resilience, however, activates the parasympathetic nervous system, which counteracts the stress response and promotes relaxation, healing, and recovery. When we engage in activities that foster resilience, such as mindfulness, exercise, or social connection, we stimulate the parasympathetic nervous system, reducing stress hormones, lowering blood pressure, and boosting our immune system.

Our gut microbiome, a vast community of bacteria residing in our digestive tract, also plays a surprising role in resilience. Research suggests that a healthy gut microbiome can enhance our ability to cope with stress and adversity by modulating the gut-brain axis, a bidirectional communication pathway between the gut and the brain. A balanced gut microbiome can influence our mood, cognitive function, and even our stress response, making us more resilient to challenges.

Genes, too, contribute to our resilience, although their influence is complex and multifaceted. While some individuals may have a genetic predisposition toward resilience, it's important to remember that genes are not destiny. Our environment, experiences, and choices play a significant role in shaping our resilience. By adopting healthy habits, fostering positive relationships, and seeking support when needed, we can nurture our resilience and overcome genetic vulnerabilities.

Understanding the science of bouncing back empowers us to take proactive steps to enhance our resilience. By engaging in activities that promote neuroplasticity, such as learning new skills, challenging ourselves, and seeking novel experiences, we can strengthen our brains' ability to adapt and thrive. By practicing mindfulness, cultivating gratitude, and fostering social connection, we can activate the parasympathetic nervous system and reduce the negative impacts of stress. By prioritizing our physical health through exercise, healthy eating, and sufficient sleep, we can bolster our bodies' resilience and enhance our overall well-being.

The science of bouncing back is a testament to the incredible resilience that resides within each of us. Our brains and bodies are not passive victims of circumstance; they are active participants in our journey toward resilience. By understanding the intricate mechanisms that underlie resilience, we can harness our own biology to overcome challenges, adapt to change, and thrive in the face of adversity. So, embrace the science of bouncing back, nurture your resilience, and unlock your full potential to live a fulfilling, empowered, and joyful life.

ᗐᗐᗐ

*Self-compassion is not a luxury; it's a necessity.
Treat yourself with the same kindness and
understanding you would offer to a dear friend,
especially during difficult times.*

FOUR

THE RESILIENCE MYTH: BUSTING COMMON MISCONCEPTIONS THAT HOLD YOU BACK.

Resilience, a word often celebrated as a personal strength and a path to success, has become shrouded in a veil of misconceptions. These myths, while seemingly harmless, can inadvertently hinder our ability to cultivate genuine resilience. Let's unravel these common misconceptions and shed light on the true nature of resilience.

One of the most pervasive myths is that resilience is an innate trait, something you're either born with or not. This notion implies that some individuals are naturally resilient while others are doomed to struggle in the face of adversity. However, resilience is not a fixed attribute; it's a skill that can be learned, developed, and strengthened over time. Just like any other skill, resilience requires practice, effort, and a willingness to learn from both successes and failures.

Another misconception is that resilient people don't experience pain or suffering. This myth portrays resilient individuals as emotionless robots who stoically endure hardships without flinching. In reality, resilient people experience the full range of human emotions, including sadness, anger, and fear. The difference lies in their ability to acknowledge and process these emotions in a healthy way, rather than letting them consume them. Resilience isn't about suppressing emotions; it's about embracing them, learning from them, and using them as fuel for growth.

The myth of the lone wolf further distorts our understanding of resilience. This misconception suggests that resilient individuals are self-reliant and independent, tackling challenges without seeking help from others. However, resilience thrives in connection and community. Resilient people understand the importance of building a strong support system, seeking guidance from mentors, and reaching out for help when needed. Vulnerability isn't a weakness; it's a strength that allows us to forge deeper connections and access the support we need to overcome challenges.

Some believe that resilience means bouncing back quickly from setbacks, as if adversity were a minor inconvenience that can be easily brushed aside. This myth overlooks the fact that healing and recovery take time. Resilient people don't rush through their pain; they allow themselves to grieve, to process, and to learn from their experiences. Bouncing back isn't about returning to the way things were; it's about emerging from adversity stronger, wiser, and more compassionate.

Another misconception is that resilience is about being positive all the time. While optimism can be a helpful tool, it's not the sole ingredient of resilience. Resilient people acknowledge the negative aspects of a situation, allowing themselves to feel the full weight of their emotions. It's through this honest appraisal of reality that they can then identify potential solutions and move forward with clarity and purpose.

The myth of the superhero further perpetuates unrealistic expectations of resilience. This misconception portrays resilient individuals as invincible, capable of overcoming any obstacle without breaking a sweat. In reality, resilience isn't about being superhuman; it's about being human. Resilient people have their limits, their vulnerabilities, and their moments of weakness. It's through acknowledging these limitations that they can then find creative solutions, seek support, and continue their journey toward resilience.

Finally, some believe that resilience is a one-and-done deal, a goal to be achieved and then checked off the list. However, resilience is a lifelong journey, a continuous process of growth, adaptation, and self-discovery. Just as life throws us new challenges, our resilience must evolve and adapt to meet those challenges. It's not about reaching a finish line; it's about embracing the journey, learning from every experience, and becoming a stronger, more resilient version of ourselves.

By debunking these common misconceptions, we can embrace a more nuanced and realistic understanding of resilience. Resilience isn't about being perfect or invincible; it's about being human. It's about acknowledging our vulnerabilities, embracing our emotions, seeking support, and learning from our experiences. It's about finding the strength to overcome challenges, the courage to face adversity, and the wisdom to grow from setbacks. Resilience is not a destination; it's a journey. And it's a journey that we can all embark on, regardless of our past experiences or current circumstances. By cultivating resilience, we empower ourselves to live more fulfilling, meaningful, and joyful lives.

ᚦᚦᚦ

Your emotions are not your enemies; they are your messengers. Learn to listen to them, understand them, and respond to them in a healthy and constructive way.

FIVE

MINDSET MATTERS: SHIFTING YOUR PERSPECTIVE TO EMBRACE CHALLENGES.

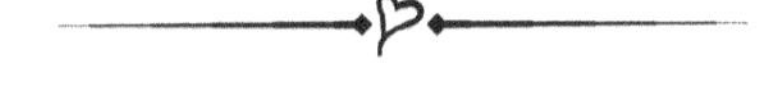

In the intricate tapestry of resilience, mindset emerges as a guiding thread, weaving its way through our thoughts, emotions, and actions. It's the lens through which we perceive the world, the filter that colors our experiences, and the compass that directs our choices. The power of mindset lies in its ability to shape our reality, influencing how we interpret challenges, setbacks, and even successes.

The concept of mindset, as explored by renowned psychologist Carol Dweck, revolves around two distinct perspectives: the fixed mindset and the growth mindset. A fixed mindset assumes that our abilities, intelligence, and talents are static and unchangeable. Individuals with a fixed mindset believe that they are either good at something or not, and that effort is futile if it doesn't yield immediate results. This perspective often leads to a fear of failure, a reluctance to take risks, and a tendency to avoid challenges that might expose perceived weaknesses.

In contrast, a growth mindset embraces the belief that our abilities are not fixed but can be developed through dedication and hard work. Individuals with a growth mindset view challenges as opportunities for learning and growth, setbacks as temporary hurdles, and effort as a path to mastery. This perspective fosters a love of learning, a resilience in the face of obstacles, and a willingness to step outside one's comfort zone.

The impact of mindset on resilience is profound. A fixed mindset can become a self-fulfilling prophecy, limiting our potential and hindering our ability to bounce back from adversity. When we believe that our abilities are fixed, we tend to give up easily when faced with challenges, fearing that our efforts will be in vain. We may also become defensive and avoid feedback, as we see it as a threat to our self-esteem. This defensive posture can prevent us from learning from our mistakes and growing from our experiences.

A growth mindset, on the other hand, fuels resilience. When we believe that our abilities can be developed, we are more likely to persevere in the face of challenges, seeking out opportunities to learn and grow. We embrace feedback as a valuable tool for improvement, and we view setbacks as temporary setbacks, not permanent failures. This resilient mindset allows us to bounce back from adversity stronger and wiser than before.

Shifting your perspective to embrace a growth mindset is a powerful step towards cultivating greater resilience. Start by challenging your fixed mindset beliefs. When you find yourself thinking "I'm not good at this" or "I'll never be able to do that," reframe those thoughts into "I'm not good at this yet, but I can learn" or "I can develop the skills I need to achieve this."

Embrace challenges as opportunities for growth. Instead of avoiding difficult tasks, see them as a chance to learn new skills, stretch your abilities, and expand your horizons. Celebrate your effort and progress, not just your accomplishments. Recognize that the journey toward mastery is just as important as the destination.

Surround yourself with people who have a growth mindset. Their positive attitude and encouragement can be contagious, inspiring you to embrace challenges and persevere in the face of setbacks. Seek out mentors who can guide you and provide constructive feedback.

Cultivating a growth mindset is not an overnight process, but it's a worthwhile journey. By shifting your perspective to embrace challenges, you unlock your full potential for growth, resilience, and success. Remember, your mindset is not a fixed trait; it's a choice. Choose to embrace a growth mindset, and watch your resilience soar.

As you embark on this journey, be patient and kind to yourself. It's okay to stumble and make mistakes. The key is to learn from those experiences and keep moving forward. Remember, resilience is not about being perfect; it's about being human. It's about embracing challenges, learning from setbacks, and continuously growing as an individual. With a growth mindset, you can transform challenges into opportunities, setbacks into stepping stones, and adversity into fuel for your personal growth.

ᗡᗡᗡ

Your values and purpose are your guiding stars. When you live in alignment with them, you tap into a wellspring of inner strength and resilience that empowers you to overcome any obstacle.

SIX

THE POWER OF SELF-COMPASSION: BEING KIND TO YOURSELF DURING TOUGH TIMES.

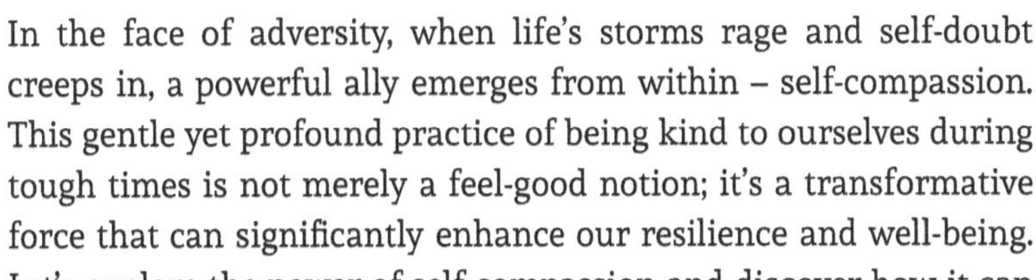

In the face of adversity, when life's storms rage and self-doubt creeps in, a powerful ally emerges from within – self-compassion. This gentle yet profound practice of being kind to ourselves during tough times is not merely a feel-good notion; it's a transformative force that can significantly enhance our resilience and well-being. Let's explore the power of self-compassion and discover how it can become a beacon of strength in our lives.

At its core, self-compassion involves treating ourselves with the same kindness, care, and understanding that we would offer to a dear friend in need. It's about acknowledging our pain and suffering without judgment or criticism, recognizing that we are all human and imperfect. Self-compassion isn't about self-pity or self-indulgence; it's about embracing ourselves with warmth, acceptance, and unwavering support.

The practice of self-compassion has its roots in ancient Buddhist teachings, where it is considered a cornerstone of emotional well-being. In recent years, it has gained recognition in the field of psychology as a powerful tool for coping with stress, anxiety, depression, and other mental health challenges. Research has shown that self-compassion can reduce anxiety, increase happiness, improve self-esteem, and enhance our ability to cope with difficult emotions.

One of the key components of self-compassion is self-kindness. This involves speaking to ourselves in a gentle, encouraging tone, offering words of comfort and support when we're struggling. Instead of berating ourselves for our mistakes or shortcomings, we can acknowledge our imperfections with understanding and acceptance. Self-kindness also means prioritizing our well-being, taking care of our physical and emotional needs, and giving ourselves permission to rest and recharge.

Another crucial aspect of self-compassion is common humanity. This involves recognizing that we are not alone in our suffering, that everyone experiences pain, disappointment, and setbacks at some point in their lives. When we connect with the shared human experience of imperfection, we can release feelings of isolation and shame, replacing them with a sense of belonging and connection.

Mindfulness, the third component of self-compassion, involves being present with our emotions without judgment or resistance. Instead of trying to suppress or avoid difficult emotions, we can observe them with curiosity and openness, acknowledging their presence without getting overwhelmed by them. Mindfulness allows us to create space between ourselves and our emotions, enabling us to respond to them in a more skillful and compassionate way.

The power of self-compassion lies in its ability to transform our relationship with ourselves. When we practice self-compassion, we cultivate a sense of inner safety and security, knowing that we have our own backs, even in the face of adversity. This inner strength empowers us to face challenges with greater courage, resilience, and optimism.

Self-compassion also helps us to break free from the cycle of self-criticism and negative self-talk. When we are kind to ourselves, we are less likely to engage in self-blame or self-deprecation. Instead, we can learn from our mistakes and move forward with greater self-acceptance and confidence.

Furthermore, self-compassion enhances our emotional resilience. When we approach difficult emotions with kindness and understanding, we are better able to regulate them and prevent them from spiraling out of control. This emotional resilience allows us to bounce back from setbacks more quickly and with less emotional distress.

The practice of self-compassion can be incorporated into our daily lives in various ways. We can start by simply noticing when we are being harsh or critical of ourselves and gently reminding ourselves to be kind. We can also engage in self-compassion exercises, such as writing a letter to ourselves from a compassionate perspective or practicing mindfulness meditation.

Additionally, we can cultivate self-compassion by surrounding ourselves with supportive people who encourage us to be kind to ourselves. We can also seek guidance from therapists or coaches who specialize in self-compassion training.

The journey toward self-compassion is a personal one, and it takes time and practice. However, the rewards are immeasurable. When we embrace self-compassion, we unlock a wellspring of inner strength, resilience, and well-being. We discover that our imperfections do not define us, and that we are worthy of love and acceptance, even when we stumble or fall. So, let us all strive to cultivate self-compassion, not as a luxury but as a necessity. By being kind to ourselves during tough times, we can navigate life's challenges with greater grace, resilience, and joy.

ϷϷϷ

Problem-solving is an art, not a science. Embrace creativity, challenge assumptions, and think outside the box to find innovative solutions to life's challenges.

SEVEN

Emotional Regulation 101. Tools for managing difficult emotions.

———♡———

Life is an emotional rollercoaster, filled with exhilarating highs and challenging lows. Difficult emotions, such as anger, sadness, fear, and anxiety, are an inevitable part of the human experience. While we often strive to avoid or suppress these emotions, they serve a valuable purpose, providing us with important information about ourselves and our environment. Learning to manage these emotions effectively is a crucial aspect of emotional regulation, a skill that can significantly enhance our resilience and well-being. Let's dive into Emotional Regulation 101 and explore a toolbox of strategies for navigating the turbulent waters of our emotional landscape.

At the heart of emotional regulation lies the ability to recognize, understand, and respond to our emotions in a healthy and constructive way. It's about acknowledging our emotions without judgment, allowing ourselves to feel them fully, and then choosing how we want to respond to them. Emotional regulation isn't about suppressing or denying our emotions; it's about harnessing their power and using them to inform our decisions and actions.

One of the most fundamental tools for emotional regulation is mindfulness. This practice involves paying attention to the present moment with curiosity and non-judgment. When we are mindful, we become aware of our emotions as they arise, without getting caught up in them or reacting impulsively. Mindfulness allows us to create space between ourselves and our emotions, enabling us to respond to them in a more skillful and intentional way.

Another valuable tool for emotional regulation is cognitive reappraisal. This involves changing the way we think about a situation in order to change the way we feel about it. For example, if we are feeling anxious about an upcoming presentation, we can reappraise the situation as an opportunity to share our knowledge and connect with others. By reframing our thoughts, we can shift our emotional response from anxiety to excitement or confidence.

Deep breathing exercises are a simple yet effective way to regulate our emotions. When we are stressed or anxious, our breathing tends to become shallow and rapid. By consciously slowing down and deepening our breath, we can activate the parasympathetic nervous system, which promotes relaxation and calmness. Deep breathing exercises can be done anytime, anywhere, making them a convenient tool for managing difficult emotions.

Physical activity is another powerful tool for emotional regulation. Exercise releases endorphins, natural mood boosters that can help to alleviate stress, anxiety, and depression. Regular physical activity can also improve sleep quality, boost energy levels, and enhance overall well-being, all of which contribute to greater emotional resilience.

Social connection plays a crucial role in emotional regulation. Talking to a trusted friend, family member, or therapist can help us to process difficult emotions, gain perspective, and receive support. Simply spending time with loved ones can also provide a sense of comfort and connection, reducing feelings of isolation and loneliness.

Creative expression can be a therapeutic outlet for emotions. Writing, painting, drawing, music, or dance can provide a safe space for us to express our feelings in a non-verbal way. Engaging in creative activities can also be a source of joy and fulfillment, promoting positive emotions and enhancing our overall well-being.

Self-care is an essential aspect of emotional regulation. Taking care of our physical and emotional needs through activities such as getting enough sleep, eating nutritious food, spending time in nature, and engaging in hobbies or activities that bring us joy can help to build our resilience and make us better equipped to handle difficult emotions.

Emotional regulation is a lifelong journey, and there is no one-size-fits-all approach. The key is to experiment with different tools and techniques to find what works best for you. Remember, emotional regulation is not about being perfect; it's about progress. Be patient and kind to yourself as you learn and grow. With practice and perseverance, you can develop the skills you need to navigate the complexities of your emotional landscape with greater ease, resilience, and joy.

ɒɒɒ

Connection and community are the lifelines of resilience. Surround yourself with people who uplift you, inspire you, and challenge you to grow.

EIGHT

FINDING YOUR INNER STRENGTH: TAPPING INTO YOUR VALUES AND PURPOSE.

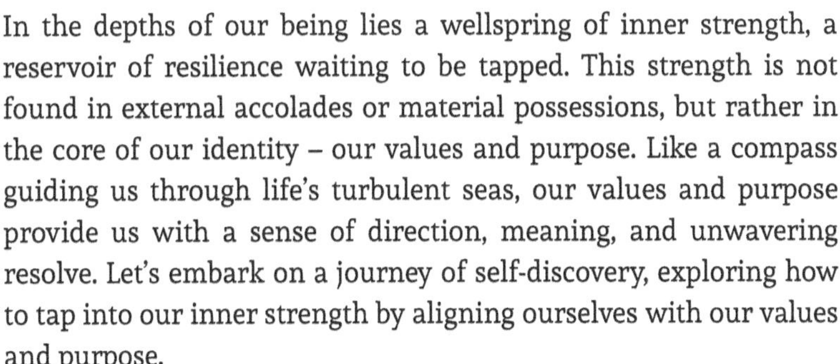

In the depths of our being lies a wellspring of inner strength, a reservoir of resilience waiting to be tapped. This strength is not found in external accolades or material possessions, but rather in the core of our identity – our values and purpose. Like a compass guiding us through life's turbulent seas, our values and purpose provide us with a sense of direction, meaning, and unwavering resolve. Let's embark on a journey of self-discovery, exploring how to tap into our inner strength by aligning ourselves with our values and purpose.

Values are the guiding principles that shape our beliefs, attitudes, and behaviors. They are the compass that points us towards what truly matters in life. Our values are not imposed upon us; they are chosen by us, reflecting our deepest convictions and aspirations. When we live in alignment with our values, we experience a sense of integrity, authenticity, and fulfillment. We feel empowered to make choices that are true to ourselves, even when faced with challenges or adversity.

Purpose, on the other hand, is our reason for being, our unique contribution to the world. It's the fire that ignites our passion, the force that drives our actions, and the legacy we leave behind. Our purpose is not something we find; it's something we create. It's an ongoing process of self-discovery, exploration, and evolution. When we live with purpose, we experience a sense of meaning, significance, and contribution. We feel motivated to make a difference, to leave our mark on the world, and to create a life that is both fulfilling and impactful.

The intersection of values and purpose is where our inner strength resides. When our actions align with our values and our purpose, we tap into a deep reservoir of resilience. We become more confident, determined, and unwavering in our pursuit of our goals. We are less swayed by external pressures or opinions, as we are grounded in our own sense of what is right and meaningful.

Finding our inner strength begins with identifying our values. Take some time to reflect on what truly matters to you. What are the principles that guide your decisions and actions? What are the qualities you admire in others? What are the causes you care deeply about? Once you have identified your values, write them down and make a conscious effort to incorporate them into your daily life.

Discovering our purpose is a more complex process, but it's a journey worth taking. Start by asking yourself what you're passionate about. What are the activities that bring you joy and fulfillment? What are the problems you want to solve? What are the skills and talents you want to share with the world? Explore different avenues, experiment with new ideas, and don't be afraid to take risks. The journey of self-discovery is often messy and unpredictable, but it's also incredibly rewarding.

Once you have identified your purpose, create a vision for your life. What do you want to achieve? How do you want to contribute to the world? Write down your vision and create a plan to make it a reality. Break down your goals into smaller, actionable steps, and celebrate your progress along the way.

Living in alignment with our values and purpose requires ongoing effort and commitment. It's not always easy to stay true to ourselves, especially when faced with challenges or adversity. However, the rewards are immeasurable. When we tap into our inner strength, we become more resilient, confident, and empowered to create the life we want to live.

Remember, our values and purpose are not static; they can evolve and change over time. As we grow and learn, our priorities may shift, and our passions may evolve. Embrace this fluidity, and allow yourself to explore new avenues and redefine your purpose as needed.

Finding our inner strength is not about becoming someone we're not; it's about embracing who we truly are. It's about living a life that is authentic, meaningful, and fulfilling. When we tap into our values and purpose, we unlock our full potential and become the best version of ourselves. So, let us all embark on this journey of self-discovery, embrace our values, pursue our purpose, and unleash our inner strength.

ϾϾϾ

Stress is an inevitable part of life, but it doesn't have to control you. Develop healthy coping mechanisms, such as mindfulness, exercise, and social connection, to manage stress and build resilience.

NINE

THE ART OF PROBLEM-SOLVING: TURNING SETBACKS INTO OPPORTUNITIES.

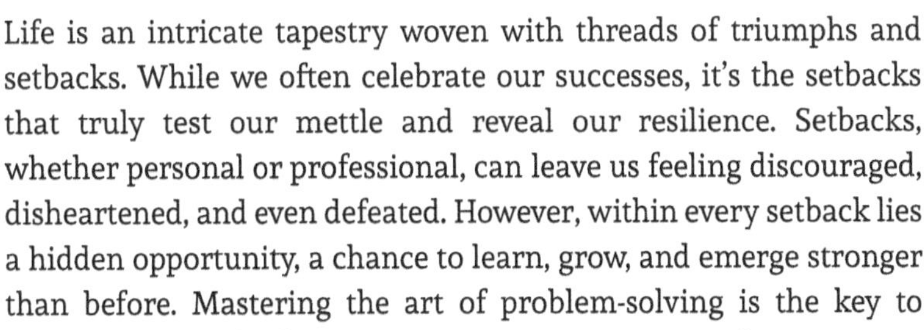

Life is an intricate tapestry woven with threads of triumphs and setbacks. While we often celebrate our successes, it's the setbacks that truly test our mettle and reveal our resilience. Setbacks, whether personal or professional, can leave us feeling discouraged, disheartened, and even defeated. However, within every setback lies a hidden opportunity, a chance to learn, grow, and emerge stronger than before. Mastering the art of problem-solving is the key to transforming setbacks into stepping stones on our path to success.

Problem-solving is not merely a skill; it's a mindset, an approach to life that embraces challenges as opportunities for growth. It's about looking beyond the surface, delving deeper into the root causes of a problem, and finding creative solutions that not only address the immediate issue but also prevent it from recurring in the future.

The first step in the art of problem-solving is to reframe our perspective. Instead of viewing setbacks as failures, we can see them as valuable feedback, as signals that something needs to change or improve. This shift in perspective allows us to approach challenges with curiosity and a willingness to learn, rather than with fear and resistance.

Once we've reframed our perspective, the next step is to define the problem clearly. What exactly is the issue at hand? What are the underlying causes? What are the potential consequences if the problem is not addressed? By clearly defining the problem, we can avoid getting sidetracked by irrelevant details and focus our energy on finding effective solutions.

Once we have a clear understanding of the problem, we can start brainstorming potential solutions. This is where creativity comes into play. Don't limit yourself to conventional thinking; explore unconventional ideas, challenge assumptions, and think outside the box. The more diverse your range of potential solutions, the more likely you are to find one that truly addresses the root of the problem.

After brainstorming, it's time to evaluate the potential solutions and choose the best course of action. Consider the pros and cons of each option, weighing the potential benefits against the risks and costs. It's also important to factor in your values and priorities. The best solution is not always the most obvious or the easiest one; it's the one that aligns with your overall goals and aspirations.

Once you've chosen a solution, it's time to implement it. This is where perseverance comes into play. Don't be discouraged by initial setbacks or obstacles; stay focused on your goal and keep moving forward. Remember, problem-solving is an iterative process. You may need to adjust your approach along the way, but as long as you keep learning and adapting, you will eventually find a solution that works.

Throughout the problem-solving process, it's important to maintain a positive attitude. Optimism can be a powerful fuel for resilience, helping us to stay motivated and hopeful even when faced with seemingly insurmountable challenges. A positive attitude can also open our minds to new possibilities and creative solutions.

The art of problem-solving is not just about finding solutions to immediate challenges; it's also about learning from our experiences and building resilience for the future. Every setback we encounter is an opportunity to learn, grow, and become better equipped to handle future challenges. By embracing a problem-solving mindset, we can transform setbacks into stepping stones on our path to success.

Remember, problem-solving is not a solo endeavor. Seek support from others, whether it's from friends, family, mentors, or colleagues. Two heads are often better than one, and collaboration can lead to more creative and effective solutions. Don't be afraid to ask for help when you need it.

Finally, celebrate your successes, no matter how small they may seem. Each step forward, each obstacle overcome, is a testament to your resilience and problem-solving skills. By acknowledging and celebrating your progress, you reinforce a positive feedback loop that further strengthens your resilience and motivates you to keep moving forward.

The art of problem-solving is a lifelong journey of learning, growth, and self-discovery. By embracing challenges as opportunities, reframing our perspectives, and seeking creative solutions, we can turn setbacks into stepping stones on our path to success.

Remember, resilience is not about avoiding problems; it's about facing them head-on, learning from them, and emerging stronger than before.

❦❦❦

Your body is your temple, your mind is your garden. Nourish them with healthy habits, such as a balanced diet, regular exercise, and sufficient sleep.

TEN

Building a Support System: The importance of connection and community.

In the intricate dance of life, we are not solitary figures twirling in isolation. We are inherently social beings, wired for connection, belonging, and community. Building a strong support system is not merely a luxury; it's a fundamental pillar of resilience, a lifeline that sustains us through life's storms and empowers us to thrive. Let's delve into the profound importance of connection and community in fostering resilience and discover how to cultivate a network of support that uplifts and empowers.

Humans are not designed to go through life alone. We thrive in the presence of others, finding solace, strength, and inspiration in our relationships. A robust support system acts as a buffer against stress, providing us with a safe space to share our burdens, seek guidance, and receive encouragement. When we feel connected and supported, we are more likely to persevere in the face of challenges, knowing that we are not alone in our struggles.

Connection and community foster a sense of belonging, a fundamental human need that is essential for our well-being. When we feel like we belong to a group or community, we experience a sense of identity, purpose, and shared values. This sense of belonging can be a powerful source of resilience, providing us with a sense of rootedness and stability during times of change or uncertainty.

A strong support system also provides us with a diverse range of perspectives and resources. When we face challenges, it can be helpful to seek advice from others who have experienced similar situations or who have expertise in relevant areas. Our support network can offer us different viewpoints, helping us to see the situation more clearly and identify potential solutions that we might not have considered on our own.

Furthermore, connection and community can provide us with emotional support, a crucial ingredient for resilience. When we are going through a difficult time, having someone to listen to us, validate our feelings, and offer words of comfort can make a world of difference. Emotional support can help us to process difficult emotions, reduce stress, and maintain a positive outlook.

Building a strong support system takes time and effort, but it's an investment that yields invaluable returns. Start by identifying the people in your life who you can trust and rely on. These may be friends, family members, mentors, colleagues, or even members of a support group or online community. Nurture these relationships by spending quality time together, offering support in return, and communicating openly and honestly.

Don't be afraid to ask for help when you need it. Many of us hesitate to reach out for support, fearing that we will be seen as weak or burdensome. However, asking for help is a sign of strength, not weakness. It takes courage to admit that we need assistance, and it opens the door for others to offer their support and expertise.

Building a support system is not just about receiving support; it's also about giving it. When we offer support to others, we not only strengthen our relationships but also enhance our own resilience. Helping others can give us a sense of purpose, boost our self-esteem, and remind us of our own strengths and capabilities.

In addition to our personal support network, it's also important to cultivate a sense of community. This can involve joining clubs, organizations, or groups that share our interests and values. Participating in community activities can provide us with a sense of belonging, purpose, and connection to something larger than ourselves.

In the digital age, online communities can also play a significant role in our support systems. Online forums, social media groups, and virtual support groups can provide a platform for connecting with others who share our experiences and challenges. However, it's important to be mindful of the potential pitfalls of online interaction, such as cyberbullying and misinformation.

Building a strong support system is a lifelong journey. As our lives evolve, so do our relationships and our needs for support. Some relationships may fade away, while new ones may blossom. Embrace the fluidity of life and be open to new connections and communities.

Remember, building a support system is not about quantity; it's about quality. It's better to have a few close, supportive relationships than a large network of superficial connections. Focus on building meaningful relationships with people who uplift you, inspire you, and challenge you to grow.

Connection and community are not just nice-to-haves; they are essential for our resilience and well-being. By building a strong support system, we create a safety net that catches us when we fall, a springboard that propels us forward, and a beacon of light that guides us through life's darkest hours. So, let us all strive to cultivate meaningful connections, foster a sense of community, and build a support system that empowers us to thrive.

ppp

Resilience at work is not about being a workaholic; it's about finding a balance between productivity and well-being. Set realistic expectations, manage your time effectively, and prioritize self-care.

ELEVEN

STRESS-BUSTING STRATEGIES: SIMPLE PRACTICES FOR DAILY RESILIENCE.

In our fast-paced, demanding world, stress has become an unwelcome companion, casting a shadow over our well-being and resilience. While we can't eliminate stress entirely, we can equip ourselves with a powerful arsenal of stress-busting strategies to navigate its turbulent waters. These simple yet effective practices can be seamlessly integrated into our daily lives, fostering resilience and empowering us to thrive amidst life's challenges.

One of the most fundamental stress-busting strategies is mindfulness. This ancient practice involves paying full attention to the present moment without judgment. By anchoring ourselves in the here and now, we can break free from the grip of worries about the future or regrets about the past. Mindfulness can be cultivated through various techniques, such as meditation, yoga, or simply taking a few minutes each day to focus on our breath and observe our surroundings. As we become more mindful, we develop a greater awareness of our thoughts and emotions, enabling us to respond to stressors with greater clarity and composure.

Another powerful stress-buster is physical activity. Exercise is not only beneficial for our physical health but also for our mental well-being. When we engage in physical activity, our bodies release endorphins, natural mood boosters that can alleviate stress, anxiety, and depression. Regular exercise can also improve sleep quality, increase energy levels, and enhance our overall resilience. Find an activity you enjoy, whether it's dancing, swimming, hiking, or simply taking a brisk walk, and make it a regular part of your routine.

Social connection is a vital component of stress management. Spending time with loved ones, engaging in meaningful conversations, and participating in social activities can provide a much-needed respite from stress. Social connection releases oxytocin, a hormone that promotes bonding and reduces stress. Nurture your relationships, reach out to friends and family, and make time for social activities that bring you joy and connection.

Creative expression can be a therapeutic outlet for stress. Whether it's painting, writing, playing music, or simply doodling, engaging in creative activities can help us to process our emotions, express ourselves authentically, and tap into our inner joy. Creative expression can also be a form of mindfulness, as it requires us to focus our attention on the present moment and engage our senses fully.

Deep breathing exercises are a simple yet effective way to calm our nervous system and reduce stress. When we are stressed, our breathing tends to become shallow and rapid. By consciously slowing down and deepening our breath, we can activate the parasympathetic nervous system, which promotes relaxation and calmness. Deep breathing exercises can be done anytime, anywhere, making them a convenient tool for managing stress on the go.

Spending time in nature has a profound impact on our stress levels. Research has shown that spending time in green spaces can lower blood pressure, reduce cortisol levels, and improve mood. Whether it's a walk in the park, a hike in the woods, or simply sitting under a tree, immersing ourselves in nature can be a restorative and rejuvenating experience.

A good night's sleep is essential for managing stress and maintaining resilience. When we are well-rested, we are better equipped to handle challenges and cope with difficult emotions. Make sleep a priority by establishing a consistent sleep schedule, creating a relaxing bedtime routine, and ensuring your sleep environment is conducive to rest.

Proper nutrition plays a crucial role in stress management. A balanced diet rich in fruits, vegetables, whole grains, and lean protein can provide our bodies with the nutrients they need to function optimally and cope with stress. Avoid processed foods, sugary drinks, and excessive caffeine, as these can exacerbate stress and disrupt sleep.

Stress management is an ongoing process, and it's important to experiment with different strategies to find what works best for you. Remember, there is no one-size-fits-all approach. What works for one person may not work for another. Listen to your body, pay attention to your emotions, and be willing to try new things. By incorporating these simple yet effective stress-busting strategies into your daily life, you can cultivate greater resilience, reduce stress, and enhance your overall well-being.

ᐅᐅᐅ

Relationships are the heart and soul of our lives. Navigate conflict with grace, build stronger bonds, and foster a resilient connection with your loved ones.

TWELVE

Healthy Habits for a Resilient You: Nourishing your body and mind.

Resilience isn't just about mental fortitude; it's a holistic state of being that encompasses our physical, emotional, and mental well-being. Nourishing our bodies and minds through healthy habits is essential for cultivating resilience and thriving in the face of life's challenges. Let's explore a tapestry of healthy habits that can empower us to become the most resilient versions of ourselves.

At the foundation of a resilient life lies a nourishing diet. The food we consume fuels our bodies and minds, providing the energy and nutrients we need to function optimally. A balanced diet rich in fruits, vegetables, whole grains, lean protein, and healthy fats provides essential vitamins, minerals, and antioxidants that support our immune system, boost our mood, and enhance our cognitive function. Avoid processed foods, sugary drinks, and excessive caffeine, as these can deplete our energy, disrupt our sleep, and exacerbate stress. By making mindful choices about what we put into our bodies, we can nourish ourselves from the inside out and build a strong foundation for resilience.

Regular exercise is another cornerstone of a healthy and resilient life. Physical activity not only strengthens our bodies but also our minds. Exercise releases endorphins, natural mood boosters that can alleviate stress, anxiety, and depression. It also improves sleep quality, enhances cognitive function, and boosts energy levels. Find an activity you enjoy, whether it's dancing, swimming, hiking, or simply taking a brisk walk, and make it a regular part of your routine. Aim for at least 30 minutes of moderate-intensity exercise most days of the week.

Sleep is often underestimated, but it's a vital component of resilience. When we get enough sleep, our bodies and minds have time to rest, repair, and recharge. Sleep deprivation, on the other hand, can impair our cognitive function, weaken our immune system, and make us more vulnerable to stress and negative emotions. Aim for 7-8 hours of quality sleep each night. Create a relaxing bedtime routine, avoid screens before bed, and create a sleep environment that is cool, dark, and quiet.

Stress management is essential for maintaining resilience. Chronic stress can take a toll on our physical and mental health, weakening our immune system, impairing our cognitive function, and increasing our risk of chronic diseases. Incorporate stress-reducing practices into your daily routine, such as mindfulness meditation, deep breathing exercises, yoga, or spending time in nature. These practices can help to calm our nervous system, reduce cortisol levels, and promote relaxation.

Cultivating a positive mindset is another key to resilience. Our thoughts and beliefs have a powerful impact on our emotions and behaviors. When we focus on the negative aspects of a situation, we can easily become overwhelmed and discouraged. However, when we choose to focus on the positive, we can find opportunities for growth and learning, even in the face of adversity. Practice gratitude, challenge negative self-talk, and surround yourself with positive and supportive people.

Social connection is a vital source of support and resilience. Strong relationships with friends, family, and community members can provide us with a sense of belonging, purpose, and meaning. Reach out to loved ones regularly, participate in social activities, and volunteer your time to a cause you care about. These connections can provide a buffer against stress, offer a listening ear, and remind us that we are not alone.

Lifelong learning is a powerful tool for resilience. Learning new skills, exploring new ideas, and expanding our knowledge can keep our minds sharp, boost our confidence, and open up new possibilities. Whether it's taking a course, reading a book, or simply engaging in stimulating conversations, make learning a lifelong habit.

Practicing self-compassion is essential for resilience. We are all human, and we all make mistakes. Instead of berating ourselves for our shortcomings, we can treat ourselves with kindness, understanding, and forgiveness. Self-compassion allows us to learn from our mistakes and move forward with greater self-acceptance and resilience.

Finally, don't be afraid to seek professional help if you're struggling. Therapists, counselors, and coaches can provide valuable support and guidance as you navigate life's challenges. There is no shame in asking for help, and seeking professional support can be a powerful step towards greater resilience and well-being.

Building a resilient life is an ongoing journey, not a destination. It requires commitment, perseverance, and a willingness to experiment and adapt. By incorporating these healthy habits into our daily lives, we can nourish our bodies and minds, cultivate inner strength, and thrive in the face of adversity. Remember, resilience is not about being perfect; it's about progress. Embrace the journey, celebrate your successes, learn from your setbacks, and never stop growing.

❦❦❦

Parenting is a journey, not a destination. Embrace the messiness, celebrate the milestones, and cultivate resilience in both yourself and your children.

THIRTEEN

RESILIENCE AT WORK: THRIVING IN A CHALLENGING PROFESSIONAL ENVIRONMENT.

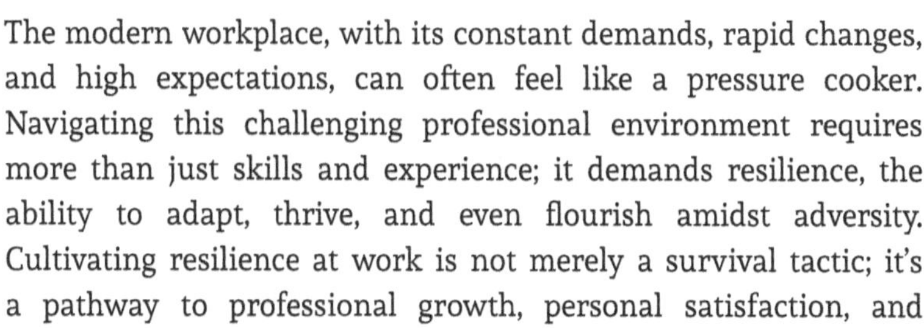

The modern workplace, with its constant demands, rapid changes, and high expectations, can often feel like a pressure cooker. Navigating this challenging professional environment requires more than just skills and experience; it demands resilience, the ability to adapt, thrive, and even flourish amidst adversity. Cultivating resilience at work is not merely a survival tactic; it's a pathway to professional growth, personal satisfaction, and sustainable success.

Resilience in the workplace isn't about becoming an emotionless workhorse, immune to stress and setbacks. It's about developing a mindset and a set of skills that enable you to navigate challenges with grace, maintain your well-being, and emerge stronger from adversity. It's about finding a balance between pushing yourself to achieve your goals and taking care of your physical and emotional needs.

One of the cornerstones of resilience at work is a positive mindset. When faced with challenges, resilient individuals tend to focus on solutions rather than dwelling on problems. They embrace a growth mindset, believing that they can learn and develop from every experience, even the difficult ones. Cultivating a positive mindset involves challenging negative self-talk, reframing setbacks as opportunities for growth, and focusing on your strengths and accomplishments.

Effective stress management is another crucial aspect of resilience at work. Chronic stress can lead to burnout, decreased productivity, and a host of physical and mental health problems. Developing healthy coping mechanisms for stress is essential for maintaining resilience. This might include practicing mindfulness, engaging in physical activity, spending time with loved ones, or pursuing hobbies and interests outside of work.

Building strong relationships with colleagues is also key to resilience in the workplace. A supportive network of colleagues can provide a sense of belonging, offer a listening ear, and offer help and encouragement during challenging times. Make an effort to connect with your colleagues, build trust, and foster a positive and collaborative work environment.

Effective communication is essential for navigating workplace challenges and building resilience. When conflicts arise, address them directly and respectfully. Clearly communicate your needs and expectations, and actively listen to the perspectives of others. Open and honest communication can help to resolve conflicts, build trust, and foster a more positive and productive work environment.

Setting realistic expectations is another important aspect of resilience at work. We often set unrealistic goals for ourselves, leading to disappointment and frustration when we don't achieve them. Instead, focus on setting achievable goals that align with your values and priorities. Break down large goals into smaller, more manageable steps, and celebrate your progress along the way.

Learning to prioritize and manage your time effectively is crucial for maintaining resilience in a demanding work environment. When we feel overwhelmed by our workload, it's easy to become stressed and burnt out. Learn to identify your most important tasks, delegate when possible, and set boundaries to protect your time and energy.

Self-care is not a luxury; it's a necessity for resilience at work. Taking care of your physical and emotional needs is essential for maintaining your energy, focus, and productivity. Make time for activities that nourish your body and mind, such as exercise, healthy eating, sleep, relaxation, and spending time with loved ones.

Embracing change is another key to resilience in the workplace. The modern work environment is constantly evolving, and being able to adapt to change is essential for success. Be open to new ideas, embrace challenges as opportunities for growth, and be willing to learn new skills and technologies.

Finally, don't be afraid to ask for help when you need it. Whether it's seeking guidance from a mentor, talking to a therapist, or simply reaching out to a trusted colleague, seeking support can be a powerful step towards greater resilience. Remember, you don't have to go through challenges alone. There are people who care about you and want to help you succeed.

Resilience at work is not about being perfect; it's about progress. It's about learning from your mistakes, adapting to change, and continuously growing as a professional. By cultivating a positive mindset, managing stress effectively, building strong relationships, communicating openly, setting realistic expectations, prioritizing self-care, and embracing change, you can thrive in even the most challenging professional environments. Remember, resilience is not a destination; it's a journey. Embrace the journey, and watch yourself blossom into a more resilient, confident, and successful professional.

ppp

Grief is a natural response to loss, not a sign of weakness. Allow yourself to feel the pain, seek support from others, and find meaning in the midst of adversity.

FOURTEEN

RESILIENCE IN RELATIONSHIPS: NAVIGATING CONFLICT AND BUILDING STRONGER BONDS.

Relationships, whether romantic, familial, or platonic, are the cornerstones of our lives, enriching us with love, support, and companionship. However, they are not without their challenges. Conflicts, misunderstandings, and differences in opinions are inevitable in any relationship. It is in navigating these turbulent waters that resilience truly shines, transforming conflicts into opportunities for growth and fostering stronger, more resilient bonds.

Resilience in relationships is not about avoiding conflict altogether; it's about approaching conflict with a constructive mindset and a willingness to find mutually beneficial solutions. It's about recognizing that disagreements are a natural part of any healthy relationship and using them as opportunities to deepen our understanding of each other and strengthen our connection.

One of the fundamental principles of resilience in relationships is effective communication. When conflicts arise, it's important to communicate our needs, feelings, and perspectives clearly and respectfully. This involves active listening, empathy, and a willingness to understand the other person's point of view. Avoid accusatory language, personal attacks, or generalizations. Instead, focus on expressing your own feelings and needs using "I" statements. For example, instead of saying "You always ignore me," you could say "I feel hurt when I don't feel heard."

Another key aspect of resilience in relationships is the ability to compromise. Rarely are conflicts black and white, with one person being entirely right and the other entirely wrong. Most disagreements involve a mix of valid perspectives and needs. Resilient couples are willing to meet in the middle, finding solutions that honor both their individual needs and the needs of the relationship. This involves flexibility, open-mindedness, and a willingness to let go of the need to be right all the time.

Forgiveness is a cornerstone of resilient relationships. Holding onto grudges and resentment can poison a relationship, creating a breeding ground for bitterness and conflict. When we forgive, we release ourselves from the burden of anger and resentment, opening the door to healing and reconciliation. Forgiveness doesn't mean condoning hurtful behavior; it means choosing to let go of the past and move forward with compassion and understanding.

Resilient relationships are built on a foundation of trust. Trust is earned over time through consistent actions that demonstrate reliability, honesty, and integrity. When we trust our partners, we feel safe to be vulnerable, share our deepest thoughts and feelings, and rely on them for support. Trust is essential for weathering the storms of life together, knowing that we have each other's backs, even when things get tough.

Resilience in relationships also involves a willingness to adapt and grow together. As individuals, we are constantly evolving, and our relationships must evolve as well. Resilient couples embrace change, recognizing that it's a natural part of life. They are willing to compromise, adjust their expectations, and find new ways to connect and support each other as their lives unfold.

Humor can be a powerful tool for navigating conflict and building stronger bonds. When tensions rise, a well-timed joke or a playful remark can diffuse the situation and remind us of the joy and connection we share. Laughter can also create a sense of shared experience and strengthen our emotional connection.

Resilience in relationships is not about being perfect; it's about progress. It's about acknowledging our imperfections, learning from our mistakes, and continuously striving to become better partners. It's about embracing challenges as opportunities for growth, communicating openly and honestly, and fostering a deep sense of trust and connection.

Remember, building resilient relationships takes time and effort. It requires patience, understanding, and a willingness to put in the work. But the rewards are immeasurable. Resilient relationships provide us with love, support, and companionship, enriching our lives in countless ways. By navigating conflict with grace, building stronger bonds, and embracing the journey of growth together, we can create relationships that stand the test of time and weather any storm.

ᐅᐅᐅ

Imperfection is not a flaw; it's a badge of courage. Embrace your unique quirks, celebrate your individuality, and let go of the need to be perfect.

FIFTEEN

RESILIENCE IN PARENTHOOD: RAISING RESILIENT CHILDREN

Parenthood is a transformative journey, filled with immense joy, profound love, and countless challenges. From sleepless nights to temper tantrums, from schoolyard dramas to teenage angst, raising children can test even the most patient and resilient of souls. But amidst the chaos and unpredictability, there is an opportunity to cultivate resilience not only in our children but also in ourselves. Resilience in parenthood is not about being a perfect parent; it's about embracing the messiness, learning from our mistakes, and finding the strength to navigate the ups and downs with grace and wisdom.

Raising resilient children starts with modeling resilience ourselves. Children learn by observing their parents, and when they see us facing challenges with courage, adapting to change with flexibility, and bouncing back from setbacks with optimism, they internalize these skills and apply them to their own lives. As parents, we can foster resilience in our children by sharing our own struggles and triumphs, teaching them problem-solving skills, and encouraging them to take healthy risks and learn from their mistakes.

Creating a nurturing and supportive environment is essential for raising resilient children. Children thrive when they feel loved, accepted, and safe to express their emotions. Encourage open communication, validate their feelings, and provide a safe space for them to share their joys and sorrows. When children feel heard and understood, they are more likely to develop a sense of self-worth and confidence, which are key components of resilience.

Teaching children coping skills is another crucial aspect of fostering resilience. When children are equipped with healthy coping mechanisms, they are better able to manage stress, anxiety, and difficult emotions. Teach them relaxation techniques, such as deep breathing exercises, mindfulness meditation, or progressive muscle relaxation. Encourage them to engage in physical activity, spend time in nature, and pursue hobbies and interests that bring them joy.

Helping children develop a growth mindset is also essential for resilience. A growth mindset is the belief that our abilities and intelligence can be developed through effort and perseverance. When children believe that they can improve through learning and practice, they are more likely to embrace challenges, persist in the face of setbacks, and ultimately achieve their goals. Encourage your children to view mistakes as opportunities for learning, praise their effort rather than just their achievements, and celebrate their progress along the way.

Building strong relationships with our children is a cornerstone of resilience in parenthood. When children feel connected to their parents, they are more likely to turn to them for support and guidance during challenging times. Make time for one-on-one interactions with each of your children, listen to their concerns with empathy and understanding, and offer unconditional love and support.

Taking care of ourselves is also crucial for resilience in parenthood. Parenting can be physically and emotionally exhausting, and it's easy to neglect our own needs in the midst of caring for our children. However, when we are well-rested, nourished, and emotionally balanced, we are better equipped to handle the challenges of parenting with grace and patience. Make time for self-care activities that replenish your energy and nurture your well-being, whether it's taking a relaxing bath, reading a book, spending time with friends, or pursuing a hobby.

Resilience in parenthood is not a solo journey; it's a shared experience. Seek support from your partner, family, friends, or a therapist if needed. Parenting can be isolating at times, and having a supportive network can make all the difference. Share your struggles, ask for help, and celebrate your victories together.

Remember, resilience is not about being perfect; it's about progress. There will be days when you feel like you're failing, when you lose your temper, or when you simply don't have the energy to be the parent you want to be. Forgive yourself for your imperfections, learn from your mistakes, and keep moving forward. By embracing the messiness of parenthood, prioritizing self-care, and cultivating resilience in ourselves and our children, we can create a family culture that thrives on challenge, celebrates growth, and embraces the beautiful chaos of life.

ᐁᐁᐁ

Your setbacks are not your failures; they are your teachers. Learn from your mistakes, adapt to change, and emerge stronger and wiser from every challenge.

SIXTEEN

RESILIENCE IN GRIEF AND LOSS: FINDING STRENGTH IN THE FACE OF ADVERSITY.

Grief and loss are inevitable threads woven into the fabric of life. They are universal experiences that touch us all at some point, leaving behind a trail of profound sorrow, heartache, and disorientation. Whether it's the death of a loved one, the end of a relationship, the loss of a job, or any other significant loss, grief can shake us to our core, leaving us feeling lost and adrift. But amidst the darkness, there is a glimmer of hope, a resilience that can emerge from the depths of our sorrow. Resilience in grief and loss is not about forgetting or moving on quickly; it's about finding the strength to navigate the pain, honoring our emotions, and ultimately finding meaning and purpose in the midst of adversity.

Grief is a complex and deeply personal experience. There is no right or wrong way to grieve, no timeline for healing, and no magic formula for finding solace. Each person's journey through grief is unique, shaped by their individual circumstances, personality, and cultural background. However, there are certain principles and practices that can help us cultivate resilience in the face of grief and loss.

One of the most important aspects of resilience in grief is allowing ourselves to feel the full range of emotions that accompany loss. This includes sadness, anger, guilt, fear, and even numbness. Suppressing or denying these emotions can prolong the healing process and prevent us from fully processing our grief. By allowing ourselves to feel our emotions, we can begin to make sense of them, integrate them into our experience, and ultimately find a way to move forward.

Seeking support from others is another crucial component of resilience in grief. Talking to a trusted friend, family member, therapist, or support group can provide a safe space for us to express our emotions, receive validation for our feelings, and gain perspective on our loss. Connecting with others who have experienced similar losses can be particularly helpful, as it can foster a sense of shared understanding and community.

Finding meaning in loss can also be a source of resilience. This doesn't mean finding a silver lining in every tragedy, but rather looking for ways that our loss can teach us, inspire us, or even transform us. We can honor the memory of our loved one by living a life that is true to our values and purpose. We can use our pain as a catalyst for personal growth, learning new skills, pursuing new passions, or helping others who are going through similar experiences.

Self-care is essential for navigating grief and loss. During times of intense emotional distress, it's easy to neglect our own needs. However, taking care of our physical and emotional well-being is crucial for maintaining our resilience. This might include eating nutritious food, getting enough sleep, exercising regularly, spending time in nature, or engaging in activities that bring us joy and relaxation.

Resilience in grief also involves learning to live with the pain of loss. Grief doesn't disappear overnight; it can linger for months or even years. Learning to live with the pain doesn't mean forgetting our loved one or pretending that everything is okay. It means finding ways to integrate our grief into our lives, creating space for both sorrow and joy. This might involve creating rituals to honor our loved one's memory, finding new ways to connect with them spiritually, or simply allowing ourselves to feel sad sometimes.

Resilience in grief is not a linear process; it's a journey with ups and downs, twists and turns. There will be days when the pain feels unbearable, when we feel like we're taking two steps back for every step forward. It's important to be patient with ourselves, to acknowledge our progress, and to celebrate our small victories.

Remember, resilience is not about forgetting or moving on; it's about finding a way to live with the pain, to honor our emotions, and to find meaning and purpose in the midst of adversity. By allowing ourselves to grieve, seeking support from others, finding meaning in loss, practicing self-care, and learning to live with the pain, we can cultivate resilience in the face of grief and loss, emerging stronger, wiser, and more compassionate than before.

Resilience is a lifelong practice, not a one-time achievement. Embrace the journey, learn from your experiences, and continuously evolve and adapt.

SEVENTEEN

Embracing Imperfection: Why "good enough" is often better than perfect.

In a world that bombards us with images of flawless beauty, impeccable success, and effortless perfection, it's easy to fall into the trap of believing that anything less than perfect is simply not good enough. This relentless pursuit of perfection can be exhausting, demoralizing, and ultimately counterproductive. But what if we were to challenge this deeply ingrained belief and embrace the radical notion that imperfection is not only acceptable but also desirable? What if we were to discover that "good enough" is often better than perfect?

Perfectionism, while often disguised as a virtue, can be a double-edged sword. On one hand, it can drive us to achieve great things, pushing us to strive for excellence and exceed our own expectations. On the other hand, it can become a crippling burden, paralyzing us with fear of failure, stifling our creativity, and robbing us of joy and satisfaction.

The pursuit of perfection is often fueled by a fear of judgment and rejection. We worry that if we don't meet impossible standards, we will be criticized, ridiculed, or deemed unworthy. This fear can lead to procrastination, anxiety, and a constant feeling of never being good enough.

Perfectionism can also be a form of self-sabotage. When we set unrealistic expectations for ourselves, we set ourselves up for disappointment and failure. We may become so focused on achieving perfection that we lose sight of the bigger picture, neglecting our relationships, our health, and our overall well-being.

Furthermore, perfectionism can hinder our creativity and innovation. When we are afraid to make mistakes, we are less likely to take risks, experiment with new ideas, or step outside of our comfort zone. We become trapped in a cycle of self-doubt and self-criticism, stifling our potential for growth and creativity.

Embracing imperfection, on the other hand, can be a liberating and empowering experience. It allows us to let go of unrealistic expectations, release the fear of judgment, and focus on the joy of the process, rather than the elusive goal of perfection.

When we embrace imperfection, we open ourselves up to new possibilities and opportunities. We become more willing to take risks, experiment with new ideas, and learn from our mistakes. We also become more compassionate towards ourselves and others, recognizing that we are all human and that imperfection is a natural part of life.

Embracing imperfection doesn't mean settling for mediocrity or abandoning our goals. It means recognizing that "good enough" is often better than perfect. Sometimes, striving for perfection can lead to diminishing returns, where the additional effort required to achieve perfection outweighs the benefits. By focusing on progress rather than perfection, we can achieve more in less time, with less stress and anxiety.

Embracing imperfection also allows us to celebrate our unique strengths and talents. Instead of comparing ourselves to others or striving to be someone we're not, we can focus on developing our own individual gifts and contributing our unique voice to the world.

In a world that constantly bombards us with messages of inadequacy, embracing imperfection is a radical act of self-love and acceptance. It's about recognizing that our worth is not determined by our achievements or our flaws, but by our inherent humanity. It's about giving ourselves permission to be imperfect, to make mistakes, and to learn and grow from those experiences.

Embracing imperfection is not an overnight transformation; it's a journey of self-discovery and self-acceptance. It requires us to challenge our deeply ingrained beliefs about perfection, to let go of the fear of judgment, and to embrace our own unique brand of imperfection. But the rewards are immeasurable. By embracing imperfection, we can cultivate greater resilience, creativity, compassion, and joy. We can live more authentically, pursue our passions with greater freedom, and create a life that is both fulfilling and meaningful. So, let us all embrace our imperfections, celebrate our unique gifts, and discover the liberating power of "good enough."

ᐅᐅᐅ

Your future is not predetermined; it's a blank canvas waiting for your brushstrokes. Create a resilient future that thrives on challenge, where setbacks become stepping stones and adversity becomes a catalyst for growth.

EIGHTEEN

THE GROWTH MINDSET: SEEING SETBACKS AS OPPORTUNITIES FOR LEARNING.

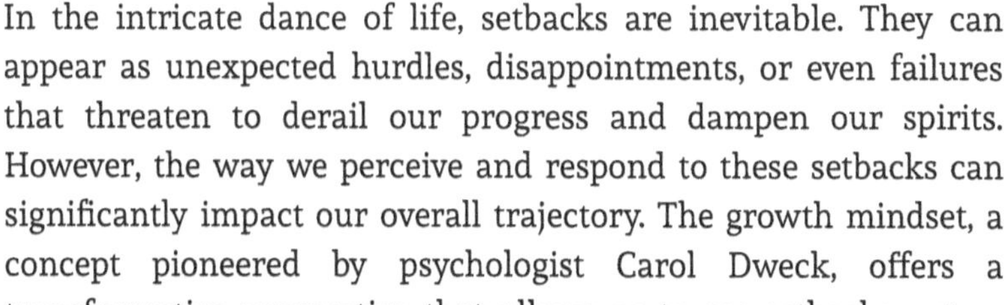

In the intricate dance of life, setbacks are inevitable. They can appear as unexpected hurdles, disappointments, or even failures that threaten to derail our progress and dampen our spirits. However, the way we perceive and respond to these setbacks can significantly impact our overall trajectory. The growth mindset, a concept pioneered by psychologist Carol Dweck, offers a transformative perspective that allows us to see setbacks not as roadblocks, but as invaluable opportunities for learning, growth, and resilience.

At its core, the growth mindset is a belief that our abilities, intelligence, and talents are not fixed but can be developed through dedication, effort, and perseverance. Individuals with a growth mindset embrace challenges, persist in the face of obstacles, learn from criticism, and view setbacks as temporary setbacks, not permanent failures. This mindset fosters a love of learning, a resilience in the face of adversity, and a willingness to step outside of our comfort zone.

The opposite of a growth mindset is a fixed mindset, which assumes that our abilities are static and unchangeable. Individuals with a fixed mindset believe that they are either good at something or not, and that effort is futile if it doesn't yield immediate results. This perspective often leads to a fear of failure, a reluctance to take risks, and a tendency to avoid challenges that might expose perceived weaknesses.

The growth mindset, on the other hand, views setbacks as an integral part of the learning process. When we encounter obstacles, our brains are challenged to adapt, to find new solutions, and to develop new skills. Each setback is an opportunity to gain valuable insights, to refine our approach, and to emerge stronger and more capable than before.

Embracing a growth mindset doesn't mean denying the pain or disappointment that accompanies setbacks. It's about acknowledging those feelings while also recognizing the potential for growth that lies within them. When we view setbacks as opportunities for learning, we are less likely to become discouraged or give up. Instead, we can use setbacks as fuel for our determination, motivating us to work harder, learn from our mistakes, and ultimately achieve our goals.

The growth mindset also encourages us to seek out challenges and embrace new experiences. Instead of sticking to what we know and avoiding anything that might expose our weaknesses, we can actively seek out opportunities to learn and grow. This might involve taking on new responsibilities at work, trying a new hobby, or learning a new skill. By stepping outside of our comfort zone, we challenge ourselves to expand our abilities and discover hidden talents.

Furthermore, the growth mindset fosters a love of learning. When we believe that we can always learn and improve, we become more curious, open-minded, and eager to explore new ideas. We become lifelong learners, constantly seeking out new knowledge and skills to enrich our lives and enhance our resilience.

Cultivating a growth mindset is not an overnight transformation, but it's a journey worth taking. Start by challenging your fixed mindset beliefs. When you find yourself thinking "I'm not good at this" or "I'll never be able to do that," reframe those thoughts into "I'm not good at this yet, but I can learn" or "I can develop the skills I need to achieve this."

Embrace challenges as opportunities for growth. Instead of avoiding difficult tasks, see them as a chance to learn new skills, stretch your abilities, and expand your horizons. Celebrate your effort and progress, not just your accomplishments. Recognize that the journey toward mastery is just as important as the destination.

Surround yourself with people who have a growth mindset. Their positive attitude and encouragement can be contagious, inspiring you to embrace challenges and persevere in the face of setbacks. Seek out mentors who can guide you and provide constructive feedback.

Remember, the growth mindset is not about being perfect; it's about progress. It's about embracing challenges, learning from setbacks, and continuously growing as an individual. With a growth mindset, you can transform setbacks into stepping stones, failures into lessons, and obstacles into opportunities. So, let go of the fear of failure, embrace the unknown, and unleash your full potential for growth and resilience. The journey may not always be easy, but it will be incredibly rewarding.

❦❦❦

You are not alone. Reach out for support when you need it, whether it's from a friend, family member, therapist, or community group.

NINETEEN

RESILIENCE AS A LIFELONG PRACTICE: CONTINUOUSLY EVOLVING AND ADAPTING.

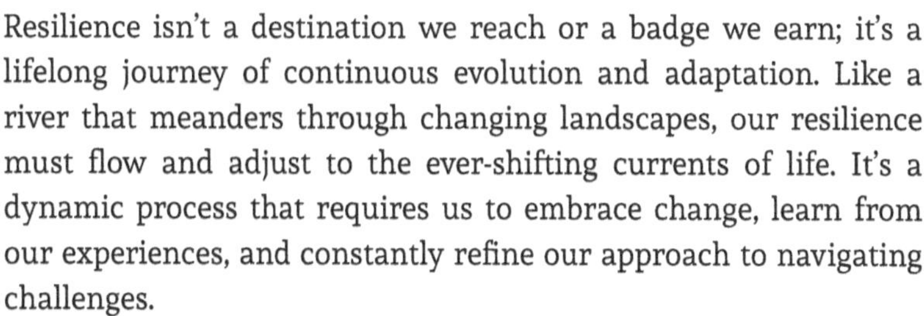

Resilience isn't a destination we reach or a badge we earn; it's a lifelong journey of continuous evolution and adaptation. Like a river that meanders through changing landscapes, our resilience must flow and adjust to the ever-shifting currents of life. It's a dynamic process that requires us to embrace change, learn from our experiences, and constantly refine our approach to navigating challenges.

The world around us is in a perpetual state of flux. From technological advancements to social shifts, from personal triumphs to unforeseen setbacks, change is the only constant. Resilience, in essence, is our ability to not only withstand these changes but to thrive amidst them. It's about embracing the unknown, adapting to new circumstances, and finding opportunities for growth and transformation in every twist and turn of life's journey.

One of the key aspects of resilience as a lifelong practice is the willingness to learn and grow. Every experience, whether positive or negative, holds valuable lessons that can shape our resilience. Setbacks, in particular, can be powerful catalysts for growth, teaching us valuable lessons about our strengths, weaknesses, and areas for improvement. Embracing a growth mindset, the belief that we can learn and improve through effort and perseverance, is essential for cultivating lifelong resilience.

Another crucial element of resilience is adaptability. Life rarely unfolds according to plan, and unexpected events can throw us off course. Resilient individuals are not rigid or inflexible; they are adaptable and resourceful, able to adjust their strategies and find new paths forward when faced with obstacles. Adaptability involves a willingness to let go of old patterns and beliefs that no longer serve us, to embrace new ideas and perspectives, and to remain open to the possibilities that lie ahead.

Resilience also requires us to cultivate a strong sense of self-awareness. By understanding our emotions, triggers, and coping mechanisms, we can better navigate challenges and respond to stressors in a healthy and constructive way. Self-awareness allows us to identify our strengths and weaknesses, set realistic expectations for ourselves, and seek support when needed. It's about knowing ourselves intimately, both our light and our shadow, so that we can respond to life's challenges with authenticity and integrity.

The practice of mindfulness can be a powerful tool for cultivating resilience as a lifelong practice. By paying attention to the present moment without judgment, we can become more aware of our thoughts, emotions, and bodily sensations. This awareness allows us to respond to stressors in a more mindful and intentional way, rather than reacting impulsively or getting caught up in negative thought patterns. Mindfulness also helps us to cultivate gratitude, appreciating the good things in our lives, even in the midst of challenges.

Another important aspect of resilience is self-care. Taking care of our physical, emotional, and mental health is essential for maintaining our resilience over time. This might include eating nutritious food, getting enough sleep, exercising regularly, spending time in nature, practicing relaxation techniques, and engaging in activities that bring us joy and fulfillment. When we prioritize self-care, we replenish our energy, reduce stress, and build a strong foundation for resilience.

Resilience is not a solitary pursuit; it thrives in connection and community. Surrounding ourselves with supportive people who believe in us and encourage us can be a powerful source of strength during challenging times. Building strong relationships with family, friends, mentors, or support groups can provide us with a safe space to share our struggles, seek guidance, and receive encouragement.

Finally, resilience is a journey of self-discovery and personal growth. It's about learning who we are, what we value, and what truly matters to us. It's about embracing our imperfections, celebrating our strengths, and continuously striving to become the best version of ourselves. As we navigate life's challenges, we evolve and adapt, becoming more resilient, compassionate, and wise.

Resilience is not a destination; it's a way of life. It's a commitment to continuous growth, adaptation, and self-discovery. By embracing change, learning from our experiences, cultivating self-awareness, practicing mindfulness, prioritizing self-care, and building strong connections, we can cultivate a resilience that will serve us well throughout our lives. Remember, resilience is not about being perfect; it's about progress. Embrace the journey, learn from your mistakes, and never stop growing.

▷▷▷

Your resilience is your superpower. Embrace it, cultivate it, and unleash your full potential to live a fulfilling, meaningful, and joyful life.

TWENTY

YOUR RESILIENT FUTURE: CREATING A LIFE THAT THRIVES ON CHALLENGE.

Your future is not a predetermined path, but a canvas waiting for your brushstrokes. It's a blank slate upon which you can paint a vibrant tapestry of experiences, achievements, and growth. A resilient future is not one devoid of challenges; it's a life that thrives on them, using them as fuel for personal and professional development. It's a life where setbacks are not seen as roadblocks but as stepping stones, where obstacles become opportunities, and where adversity becomes a catalyst for transformation.

Creating a resilient future begins with a shift in perspective. It's about embracing a growth mindset, the belief that our abilities and intelligence can be developed through dedication and hard work. When we adopt a growth mindset, we view challenges as opportunities to learn and grow, setbacks as temporary hurdles, and effort as a path to mastery. This mindset empowers us to take risks, step outside of our comfort zone, and pursue our goals with unwavering determination.

One of the key components of a resilient future is a strong sense of purpose. When we have a clear vision of what we want to achieve and why it matters to us, we are more likely to persevere in the face of challenges. Our purpose gives us a sense of direction, meaning, and motivation, propelling us forward even when the going gets tough. Take some time to reflect on your values, your passions, and your aspirations. What kind of impact do you want to make on the world? What legacy do you want to leave behind? By defining your purpose, you create a compass that guides you towards a resilient future.

Building strong relationships is another crucial aspect of a resilient future. We are social beings, and our connections with others play a vital role in our well-being and resilience. Cultivate meaningful relationships with family, friends, mentors, and colleagues who support you, encourage you, and challenge you to grow. Surround yourself with positive and uplifting people who believe in your potential and inspire you to be your best self.

Resilience also requires us to take care of our physical and mental health. Our bodies and minds are interconnected, and when one is out of balance, the other suffers. Prioritize sleep, exercise, and healthy eating. Engage in activities that reduce stress, such as mindfulness meditation, yoga, or spending time in nature. Take breaks when needed, and don't be afraid to ask for help when you're feeling overwhelmed.

Embracing change is a hallmark of a resilient future. The world around us is constantly evolving, and our ability to adapt to change is crucial for our success and well-being. Be open to new ideas, perspectives, and experiences. Challenge your assumptions, step outside of your comfort zone, and embrace the unknown with curiosity and a willingness to learn. Remember, change is not always comfortable, but it is often necessary for growth.

Resilience also involves developing a toolbox of coping skills for dealing with stress and adversity. This might include practicing relaxation techniques, such as deep breathing exercises or progressive muscle relaxation. It might also involve developing problem-solving skills, learning to manage your emotions effectively, and seeking support from others when needed. The more tools you have in your toolbox, the better equipped you will be to handle whatever life throws your way.

Another important aspect of a resilient future is continuous learning and growth. The world is constantly changing, and so are we. To stay ahead of the curve and maintain our resilience, we need to constantly learn and adapt. This might involve taking courses, reading books, attending workshops, or simply engaging in stimulating conversations with others. Lifelong learning not only expands our knowledge and skills but also keeps our minds sharp and our spirits engaged.

Finally, a resilient future is about embracing the journey, not just the destination. It's about finding joy and meaning in the process of growth and learning, not just in achieving our goals. Celebrate your successes, no matter how small they may seem, and learn from your setbacks. Remember, resilience is not about being perfect; it's about progress. It's about embracing challenges, learning from our experiences, and continuously evolving into the best version of ourselves.

By cultivating a growth mindset, defining your purpose, building strong relationships, taking care of your health, embracing change, developing coping skills, and committing to lifelong learning, you can create a resilient future that thrives on challenge. This future is not a utopian ideal, but a realistic and achievable goal. It's a future where you are not only able to withstand life's storms but to use them as fuel for your personal and professional growth. It's a future where you embrace challenges as opportunities, setbacks as stepping stones, and adversity as a catalyst for transformation. It's a future where you live a life that is not only successful but also meaningful, fulfilling, and resilient.

$$\triangleright\triangleright\triangleright$$

Remember, you are stronger than you think. You have within you the power to overcome any challenge and create a life that thrives on resilience.

TWENTY-ONE
SUMMARY

Resilience: Your Ultimate Life Compass

Life is a symphony of experiences, both harmonious and discordant. It is in navigating the inevitable challenges and setbacks that we truly discover our strength, our adaptability, and our capacity for growth. Resilience, the art of bouncing back from adversity, is not a mere trait; it's a dynamic and ever-evolving skill that empowers us to thrive amidst life's storms.

We began our journey by demystifying resilience, revealing its true essence as the ability to navigate life's challenges with grace, courage, and an unyielding spirit. It is not about avoiding or denying difficulties, but rather about embracing them as opportunities for growth and transformation.

We explored the resilience spectrum, recognizing that our resilience level fluctuates throughout life, influenced by various factors like our experiences, mindset, support system, and physical well-being. By understanding where we fall on this spectrum, we can gain valuable insights into our strengths and areas for growth, empowering us to cultivate greater resilience.

Delving into the science of bouncing back, we discovered the remarkable ways in which our brains and bodies are wired for resilience. Neuroplasticity, the brain's ability to reorganize itself, allows us to reframe our experiences and find meaning in adversity. The intricate dance between stress and resilience involves not only our brains but also our bodies, with the parasympathetic nervous system playing a crucial role in promoting relaxation and recovery.

We debunked common myths surrounding resilience, recognizing that it is not an innate trait but a skill that can be learned and developed. Resilient people are not immune to pain or suffering; they simply possess the tools to navigate those emotions in a healthy way. Resilience thrives in connection and community, not in isolation. It is a lifelong journey, not a one-time achievement.

Our exploration of mindset revealed its profound impact on resilience. A growth mindset, the belief that our abilities can be developed through effort and perseverance, fuels resilience by encouraging us to embrace challenges, learn from setbacks, and persist in the face of adversity. By shifting our perspective and adopting a growth mindset, we can unlock our full potential for growth, resilience, and success.

The power of self-compassion emerged as a guiding light in our journey towards resilience. By treating ourselves with kindness, understanding, and acceptance, we cultivate a sense of inner safety and security that empowers us to face challenges with greater courage and optimism. Self-compassion helps us break free from the cycle of self-criticism and negative self-talk, fostering a more positive and empowering relationship with ourselves.

Emotional regulation, the ability to manage difficult emotions effectively, is another essential skill for resilience. Through mindfulness, cognitive reappraisal, deep breathing exercises, physical activity, social connection, creative expression, and self-care, we can learn to navigate the turbulent waters of our emotional landscape with greater ease and resilience.

We delved into the importance of values and purpose in finding our inner strength. When we live in alignment with our values and pursue our purpose, we tap into a deep reservoir of resilience that empowers us to overcome challenges and live a more meaningful and fulfilling life.

The art of problem-solving emerged as a key tool for turning setbacks into opportunities. By reframing our perspective, clearly defining the problem, brainstorming solutions, evaluating options, implementing our chosen course of action, maintaining a positive attitude, and seeking support from others, we can transform challenges into stepping stones on our path to success.

Building a strong support system is crucial for resilience. Connection and community provide us with a sense of belonging, emotional support, diverse perspectives, and valuable resources. By nurturing our relationships, asking for help when needed, and giving back to our communities, we can create a network of support that uplifts and empowers us.

Resilience in various aspects of life, from work to relationships to parenthood, requires us to adapt our strategies and cultivate specific skills. In the workplace, resilience involves a positive mindset, effective stress management, strong relationships, open communication, realistic expectations, time management, self-care, and embracing change. In relationships, resilience involves effective communication, compromise, forgiveness, trust, adaptability, humor, and a willingness to grow together. In parenthood, resilience involves modeling resilience, creating a nurturing environment, teaching coping skills, fostering a growth mindset, building strong relationships, and prioritizing self-care.

Finally, we explored resilience in grief and loss, recognizing that it is a journey of healing, growth, and finding meaning in the midst of adversity. By allowing ourselves to feel our emotions, seeking support, finding meaning in loss, practicing self-care, and learning to live with the pain, we can emerge from grief stronger, wiser, and more compassionate.

Resilience is not a destination but a lifelong practice of continuous evolution and adaptation. It requires us to embrace change, learn from our experiences, cultivate self-awareness, practice mindfulness, prioritize self-care, and build strong connections. By integrating these practices into our daily lives, we can create a resilient future that thrives on challenge, where setbacks become stepping stones and adversity becomes a catalyst for growth. Remember, resilience is not about being perfect; it's about progress. Embrace the journey, celebrate your strengths, learn from your challenges, and never stop growing.

ᐅᐅᐅ

Citation And References

This book represents the culmination of extensive research and meticulous analysis, incorporating a diverse range of sources, including numerous books, scholarly studies, and personal experiences. Additionally, I have scoured various websites to gather relevant information and data essential for the compilation of this work. I have taken every precaution to ensure the accuracy of the information presented and have diligently cited all sources to acknowledge their contributions.

Despite these efforts, the possibility of inadvertent errors remains. I deeply value the insights of my readers and appreciate any feedback that can help identify and rectify such inaccuracies. I encourage you to bring any discrepancies to my attention.

Your feedback is not only welcome but crucial, as it will aid in correcting current editions and enhancing the content of future ones. I am committed to maintaining the highest standards of accuracy and reliability in my work and thank you for your support and understanding.

Additionally, I firmly uphold the principle of freedom of speech and expression as guaranteed under Article 19(1)(a) of the Constitution of India, and I respect the diverse viewpoints and expressions of all readers.

ᖚᖚᖚ

Other Books Of The Author

1. Empowering Minds: A Journey into Women's Self-Discovery and Power
2. The Dynamics of Motivation: Catalyzing Thought into Action
3. Meditation and Mental Well Being: The Path to Inner Peace and Clarity
4. The Psychology of Child Education: Nurturing Future Generations
5. Ethical Enlightenment: A Modern Guide to Living with Integrity
6. Voices of Empowerment: Stories of Women Rising Against Odds
7. Social Psychology in Everyday Life: Understanding Human Connections
8. The Essence of Motivational Speaking: Inspiring Change in Others
9. Balancing Acts: Women, Work, and the Will to Lead
10. Guiding with Grace: Raising Children with Compassion and Awareness
11. The Power of Positive Aging: Embracing Life After Fifty
12. Building Resilient Communities: Social Work in Action
13. The Ethical Educator: Principles for Teaching and Learning
14. From Insight to Impact: Social Psychology for a Better World
15. The Ethics of Empathy: A Guide to Ethical Living
16. The Science of Empowering the Self: Navigating Life's Challenges with Psychological Wisdom
17. The Mindful Conscious Leader: Meditation Techniques for Modern Management
18. Pioneering Spirit: Women's Pathways to Leadership and Empowerment
19. Feeling to Healing: The Role of Emotional Intelligence in Child Development
20. Transformative Talks and Words of Inspiration: Insights into Motivational Oratory

Bhajan

101. Pilgrimage of the Soul: Spiritual Journeys in India

❦❦❦

Contact

Dr. Minakshi Bansal
Social Activist
Ahmedabad, Gujarat, Bharat
minakshiindiag20@yahoo.com

❦❦❦

|| LOKAHA SAMASTHAHA SUKHINO BHAVANTU ||

www.ingramcontent.com/pod-product-compliance
Lightning Source LLC
Chambersburg PA
CBHW021211130726
47988CB00002B/607